I0117676

Company Pioneer Electric Power, Printers and Binders
Hestmark

Specifications and Contract for a Masonry Dam and Spillway

Company Pioneer Electric Power, Printers and Binders Hestmark

Specifications and Contract for a Masonry Dam and Spillway

ISBN/EAN: 9783337402327

Printed in Europe, USA, Canada, Australia, Japan

Cover: Foto ©Andreas Hilbeck / pixelio.de

More available books at **www.hansebooks.com**

Pioneer Electric Power Co.

OGDEN, UTAH.

SPECIFICATIONS AND CONTRACT

—FOR A—

MASONRY DAM AND SPILLWAY.

OCTOBER. 1896.

OGDEN, UTAH;
HESTMARK & WILCOX,
PRINTERS AND BINDERS.

. . ADVERTISEMENT . .

OFFICE OF THE PIONEER ELECTRIC POWER COMPANY,

OGDEN. UTAH.

Sealed Proposals Will be received at this office until November 16th, 1896, and then publicly opened, for furnishing all material and labor required in the construction of a masonry dam and spillway about 400 feet long and 60 feet high, to be built across the Ogden River in Ogden Canyon, Utah, about six miles from the city of Ogden.

Bids are requested on three distinct plans, viz:

PLAN A.—A rubble masonry dam of the usual type.

PLAN B.—A concrete dam consisting of piers connected by concrete arches.

PLAN C.—A combination dam, consisting of concrete piers with a steel plate facing.

Each bid is to be accompanied by a certified check for $5,000.

A bond for $50,000, with satisfactory sureties, will be required for the faithful performance of the contract.

Bidders, before submitting proposals, must make a careful and thorough examination, in person, of the site of the dam and spillway.

Plans and Specifications and Instructions to Bidders may be obtained on application to the undersigned at this office.

The right is reserved to reject any or all bids and to waive any informalities in the same.

C. K. BANNISTER,

Chief Engineer.

INSTRUCTIONS TO BIDDERS.

All bids must be made in triplicate upon printed forms to be obtained at this office, and to be accompanied by a copy of this advertisement and these specifications.

When firms bid, the individual names of the members should be written out and should be signed in full, giving the Christian names; but the signers may, if they choose, describe themselves in addition, as doing business under a given name and style as a firm.

The place of residence of every bidder, with post-office address, county and state, district or territory, must be given after his signature, which must be written in full.

All prices must be written as well as expressed in figures.

Payments will be made upon monthly estimates, but a percentage of fifteen percentum will be retained from each payment until the completion of the contract.

All signatures must be witnessed.

The contract which the bidder and sureties promise to enter into shall be, in its general provisions, in the form adopted by The Pioneer Electric Power Company and furnished herewith. Parties making bids are to be understood as accepting the terms and conditions contained in such form of contract.

Reasonable grounds for assuming that a bidder is interested in more than one bid for the same item will cause the rejection of all bids in which he is supposed to be interested.

The bidder must satisfy The Pioneer Electric Power Company of his ability to furnish the materials and of his skill to perform the work for which he bids.

Transfers of contracts, or of interests in contracts, will not be permitted, without the written consent of the Chief Engineer.

It is to be clearly understood that the prices bid are to cover all expenses of every kind that may be incurred in the construction and completion of the work in accordance with the specifications and plans, and such modifications of them as may be made.

All blank spaces in the proposal must be filled in, but no change shall be made in the phraseology of the proposal, or additions to the items.

Any one signing a proposal as agent of another, or others, must file with it legal evidence of his authority to do so.

A contract will not be awarded to a corporation until it shall have furnished satisfactory evidence of its legal capacity to enter into the same.

No advantage shall be taken of any error or omission in the accompanying specifications, as full information will be given upon application.

The envelope containing proposal must be sealed and endorsed "Proposal for Building Dam in Ogden Canyon" and addressed to "C. K. Bannister, Chief Engineer of The Pioneer Electric Power Company, Ogden. Utah."

Bidders, before submitting proposals, must make a careful and thorough examination in person of the Dam site and satisfy themselves as to character of material to be moved and facilities for obtaining materials used in construction.

Each bid is to be accompanied by a certified check for Five Thousand ($5,000.00) Dollars, payable to the Treasurer of The Pioneer Electric Power Company, said check to be returned to the bidder unless he fail to execute the contract, should it be awarded to him. A bond for Fifty Thousand ($50,000.00) Dollars will be required for the faithful performance of the contract, the sureties on the same to be satisfactory to the Executive Committee of the Board of Directors of said Company. The person or persons to whom the contract may be awarded will be required to appear at this office, with the sureties offered by him or them, and execute the contract within ten days (including Sunday) from the date of notification of such award; and in case of failure or neglect to do so, he or they will be consider as having abandoned it, and the check accompanying the proposal shall be *forfeited* to The Pioneer Electric Power Company.

Plans can be seen and forms of proposal and contract obtained at the office of the Chief Engineer, Ogden, Utah.

The Pioneer Electric Power Company reserves the right to reject any or all bids, and to waive any informality in the bids received.

A copy of the advertisement, Instructions to Bidders and Specifications will be attached to the contract and form a part of it.

The successful bidder shall at once upon the award of the contract, furnish The Pioneer Electric Power Company the address to which mail or telegraphic communications to him should be sent.

For the purpose of comparison of bids, the following quantities will be used:

PLAN A.

All Masonry Dam.

MASONRY—

Rubble masonry, dam	37,200 cu. yds.			
" overflow weir	1,700 "	38,900 cu. yds.		
Cut stone masonry, coping	115 " "			
" " " overflow weir	500 " "	615 " "		
	Total masonry	39,515 " "		

EXCAVATION—

Earth excavation (with slopes 1 to 1)	33,700 "	
Rock excavation (sides of canyon)	2,350 " "	
Iron fence	826 lin. ft.	
Waste channel		
Rock excavation	10,000 " "	

PLAN B.

Concrete with Arches and $\frac{1}{4}$-inch Steel Plate Facing.

MASONRY—

Concrete dam:

6 piers 2 abutments	18,500 cu. yds.	
arches (complete)	7.500 " "	26,000 cu. yds.
overflow weir,		1,700 " "

Total concrete,	27,700 cu. yds.

Cut stone masonry, coping,	115 cu. yds.	
" " " overflow weir,	500 " "	615 " "

Total masonry,	28,315 cu. yds.
Steel Plate Face,	350.000 lbs.

EXCAVATION—

Earth excavation. top 14 ft.,
(with slopes 1 to 1), 14,830 cu. yds.

Earth excavation, in vertical trenches,	12,720 " "	—27,550 cu. yds.
Rock excavation, (sides of canyon),		2,350 " "
Iron Fence,		820 lin. feet.
Waste channel, rock excavation,		10,000 cu. yds.

PLAN C.

Concrete Piers with Steel Face.

MASONRY—

Concrete, 7 piers and 2 abutments,	21,732 cu. yds.	
concrete toe,	3,196 " "	
arch roadway.	480 " "	

Total in dam,	25,408 cu. yds.
Overflow weir,	1.700 " "

Total concrete,	27,108 " "

Cut stone masonry coping.   115 cu. yds.

      overflow weir, 500 "   "

        Total cut stone masonry,   615 "   "

          Total masonry,   27,723 "   "

Steel Plate Face:

    steel plates, butt straps and rivets,   686,103 lbs.

    anchorage at abutments,   113,245 "

    anchorage at piers and toe,   10,692 "

Steel in roadway:

    I beams in roadway,   38,612 "

    buckle plates.   23,760 "

        Total steel,   872,412 lbs.

EXCAVATION—

Earth excavation, top 14 ft., slopes 1 to 1,   15,000 cu. yds.

Earth excavation, in vertical trenches.   10,500 "   "

        Total earth excavation,   25,500 cu. yds.

Rock excavation,   2,350 "   "

Iron fence.   820 lin. feet.

Waste channel, rock excavation.   10,000 cu. yds.

. . PROPOSAL . .

—TO—

The Pioneer Electric Power Company

—FOR—

BUILDING A MASONRY DAM AND SPILLWAY
ACROSS THE OGDEN RIVER IN OGDEN CANYON, UTAH.

The undersigned hereby declare that he ha carefully examined the annexed Instructions to Bidders, Form of Contract, and Specifications. and the drawings therein referred to, and made an inspection of the sites of the proposed dam and spillway, and will provide all necessary machinery, tools, apparatus, and other means of construction, and will do all the work and furnish all the materials called for by said Contract and Specifications, and the plans and drawings therein referred to, subject to all the conditions and requirements thereof and of your Instructions to Bidders, copies of all of which are hereto attached and, so far as they relate to this proposal, are made a part of it, and subject to the requirements under them of the Engineer, for the following sums, to-wit:

PLAN A.

ALL MASONRY DAM.

(a)   For the earth excavation required for the foundation of the dam, slopes one to one including all timber necessary for shoring and bracing, and all labor and material necessary for pumping and draining, as hereinafter specified, and including the refilling with approved material of all spaces in the excavation not occupied by the masonry, the sum of......... .... dollars, $......... ..... . per cu. yd.

(b)   For the rock excavation required for the foundation and sides of the dam, and all work incidental thereto, the sum of .... :......... ... . dollars, $ ...., per cu. yd.

(c)   For the earth excavation required for the foundation of the overflow weir and in making a channel for the waste water from the overflow weir, and all work incidental thereto, the sum of .... dollars, $ .... , per cu. yd.

(d)   For the rock excavation required for the foundation of the overflow weir and in making a channel for the waste water from the overflow weir, and all work incidental thereto. the sum of .... dollars, $ ...., per cu. yd.

(e)   For the rubble masonry in the dam and overflow weir, to comprise all the masonry (excepting only such cut dimension stone masonry as may be ordered for copings, etc., and such concrete masonry and neat cement as may be required for leving up the bedrock and joining it to the dam (as hereinafter specified, and all work incidental thereto, the sum of .... dollars, $ ...., per cu. yd.

(f)   For concrete in place, made with Portland cement, sand and broken stone, in the proportions of one, two and four by volume, as hereinafter specified, together with all work incidental thereto, the sum of .... dollars, $ .... , per cu. yd.

(g)   For concrete in place, made with Portland cement, sand and broken stone, in the proportions of one, three and five by volume, as hereinafter specified, together with all work incidental thereto, the sum of .... - .... dollars, $ ...., per cu. yd.

(h)   For Portland cement, to be used neat when ordered by the Engineer, per barrel of four hundred pounds, the sum of .... dollars. $ ...._____ per bbl.

(j)   For cut dimension stone masonry laid in Portland cement mortar, as hereinafter specified, to be used for copings and the crest of the overflow weir, etc., the sum of .... dollars, $ ...., per cu. yd.

10

(k) For ornamental wrought iron or steel railing, four feet high, for roadway, rivited up in place, the sum of ....dollars, $............ ..., per lin. ft.

(l) For all extra work done by the written order of the Engineer, its actual reasonable cost to the Contractor, as determined by the Engineer. plus fifteen per cent. of said cost.

PLAN B.

DAM WITH PIERS AND CONCRETE ARCHES.

(a) For earth excavation with sloping sides, slopes 1 to 1, required for the foundation of the dam, including all timber necessary for shoring and bracing, and all labor and material necessary for pumping, as hereinafter specified, and including the refilling with approved material of all spaces in the excavation not occupied by the masonry and steel, the sum of.............. .... dollars, $ ..., per cu. yd.

(b) For earth excavation in vertical trenches, required for the foundation of the dam, including all timber necessary for shoring and bracing, and all labor and material necessary for pumping and draining, as hereinafter specified, and including the refilling with approved material of all spaces in the excavation not occupied by masonry and steel, the sum of.............. . . ..dollars, $............ ...., per cu. yd.

(c) For the rock excavation required for the foundation and sides of the dam. and all work incidental thereto, the sum of ....dollars, $...... ... ., per cu. yd.

(d) For the earth excavation required for the foundation of the overflow weir and in making a channel for the waste water from the overflow weir, and all work incidental thereto. the sum of ... ,.......... .... _____ ....dollars. $......... ...., per cu. yd.

(e) For the rock excavation required for the foundation of the overflow weir and in making a channel for the waste water from the overflow weir, and all work incidental thereto, the sum of............ ....dollars. $..... ... ... , per cu. yd.

(f) For concrete in place,· made with Portland cement, sand and broken stone, in the proportions of one, two and four by volume, as hereinafter specified, together with all work incidental thereto, the sum of..dollars,

$.............., per cu. yd.

(g) For concrete in place, made with Portland cement, sand and broken stone, in the proportion of one, three and five by volume, as hereinafter specified, together with all work incidental thereto, the sum of..dollars,

$ ...., per cu. yd.

(h) For Portland cement, to be used neat where ordered by the Engineer, per barrel of four hundred pounds, the sum of ....dollars, $................, per bbl.

(j) For steel plate work for the facing, including butt straps, angle irons and angle bracing, riveted in place, including field rivets, the sum of...dollars, $............. per pound of finished material.

(k) For cut dimension stone masonry, laid in Portland cement mortar, as hereinafter specified, to be used for copings, the crest of the overflow weir, etc., the sum of............................... ....dollars, $..............., per cu. yd.

(l) For ornamental wrought iron or steel railing, four feet high, for roadway, riveted up in place, the sum of................ ....dollars, $..............., per lin. ft.

(m) For all extra work done by the written order of the Engineer, its actual reasonable cost to the Contractor, as determined by the Engineer, plus fifteen per cent of said cost.

PLAN C.

COMBINATION DAM WITH CONCRETE PIERS AND A STEEL PLATE FACING.

(a) For earth excavation with sloping sides, slopes 1 to 1, required for the foundation of the dam, including all timber necessary for shoring and bracing, and all labor and material necessary for pumping, as hereinafter specified, and including the refilling with approved material of all spaces in the excavation not occupied by the masonry and steel, the sum of............

....dollars, $............ .... , per cu. yd.

(b)   For earth excavation in vertical trenches, required for the foundation of the dam, including all timber necessary for shoring and bracing, and all labor and material necessary for pumping and draining, as hereinafter, specified, and including the refilling with approved material of all spaces in the excavation not occupied by masonry and steel, the sum of............ ....

....dollars, $............ . per cu. yd.

(c)   For the rock excavation required for the foundation and sides of the dam, and all work incidental thereto, the sum of .... dollars, $............ , per cu. yd.

(d)   For the earth excavation required for the foundation of the overflow weir and in making a channel for the waste water from the overflow weir, and all work incidental thereto, the sum of .... dollars, $............ , per cu. yd.

(e)   For the rock excavation required for the foundation of the overflow weir and in making a channel for the waste water from the overflow weir, and all work incidental thereto, the sum of .... dollars, $............ , per cu. yd.

(f)   For concrete in place, made with Portland cement, sand and broken stone, in the proportions of one, two and four by volume, as hereinafter specified, together with all work incidental thereto, the sum of............ ....dollars, $............ , per cu. yd.

(g)   For concrete in place, made with Portland cement, sand and broken stone, in the proportions of one, three and five by volume, as hereinafter specified, together with all work incidental thereto, the sum of............ .... dollars, $............ . per cu. yd.

(h)   For Portland cement, to be used neat where ordered by the Engineer, per barrel of four hundred pounds, the sum of ....dollars, $............ .... , per bbl.

(j)   For steel plate work for the facing, including butt straps, angle irons, I beams, buckle plates and angle bracing, riveted in place, including field rivets, the sum of.............. .... dollars, $............. , per pound, of finished material.

(k)   For cut dimension stone masonry, laid in Portland cement mortar, as hereinafter specified, to be used for copings, the the crest of overflow weir, etc., the sum of...... .. ..dollars, $............... , per cu. yd.

(l)   For ornamental wrought iron or steel railing, four feet high, for roadway, riveted up in place, the sum of.......... ....- ....dollars. $ ..., per lin. ft.

(m)   For all extra work done by written order of the Engineer, the actual reasonable cost to the Contractor, as determined by the Engineer, plus fifteen per cent. of said cost.

———

Accompanying this Proposal is a certified check for Five Thousand ($5,000.00) Dollars, which it is agreed shall become the property of The Pioneer Electric Power Company, if, in case this Proposal shall be accepted by the Board of Directors of said Company, in whole, or in such part as will include the building of a masonry dam and spillway, the undersigned shall fail to execute a contract with said Company under the conditions of this Proposal within the time provided for in the Instruction to Bidders, otherwise said check shall be returned to the undersigned.

No stockholder of the Company and no person in any office or employment of the Company is directly or indirectly interested in this Proposal, nor in any contract which may be made under it; nor in any expected profits to arise therefrom, and this proposal is made in good faith. without collusion or connection with any other person bidding for the same work.

If the contract is awarded to the undersigned, the work shall be commenced within fifteen days after the contract is signed; and the work shall be fully completed on or before the

14

_____day of_____, 189___ .

and time and punctuality shall constitute an essential part of this agreement.

For each and every day that the work shall remain unfinished from and after the date herein fixed for its completion. The Pioneer Electric Power Company may deduct and retain out of the money which may be due or become due to the undersigned, under this agreement, the sum of Fifty Dollars. ($50.00), as liquidated damages that the said Company will suffer by reason of the failure of the undersigned to complete the work within the time agreed.

(SIGNATURE)

_____

_____

_____

Names of Members of Firm.

_____

_____

_____

If corporation, sign by President and Secretary and affix seal of Company.

The Pioneer Electric Power Company

CONTRACT AND SPECIFICATIONS

—FOR—

BUILDING A MASONRY DAM AND SPILLWAY
ACROSS THE OGDEN RIVER, IN OGDEN CANYON, UTAH.

This Agreement, Made and concluded this............
....day of........ ... .,
in the year A. D. one thousand, eight hundred and ninety........
...., between The Pioneer Electric Power Company,
a corporation of the State of Utah, by its President and Secre-
tary, of the first part, and .... : ....
of.......... ... .: ....
in the State of.............. . . . .
of the second part, WITNESSETH:—

A.   That for and in consideration of payments and agreements
hereinafter mentioned, to be made and performed by the said
party of the first part, and under the penalty expressed in the
bond bearing even date with these presents and hereunto annexed, the said party of the second part agrees with the said
party of the first part to commence the work herein required

Commence-
ment
of Work. to be done within fifteen days after the signing of this contract, and to proceed with the work in such order and at such
times, points, and seasons, and with such force as may, from
time to time, be directed by the Engineer, and at his own
proper cost and expense to do all the work and furnish all the
materials called for by this agreement, in the manner and under the conditions hereinafter specified.

And the said party of the second part hereby agrees to complete all the work called for under this agreement, in all parts and requirements and in full conformity with the plans and specifications, on or before the .... day of .... , one thousand eight hundred

Completion of Work.

and ninety .... , provided, however, that the party of the first part shall have the right at its discretion to extend the time for said completion of the work. It is further agreed that the permitting of said party of the second part to go on and finish said work after the time specified for its completion shall not operate as a waiver of any of the rights of said party of the first part under this contract.

B.

Referee.

To prevent all disputes and litigation, it is further agreed by and between the parties to this contract, that the Chief Engineer of The Pioneer Electric Power Company (meaning thereby the individual at any time holding the position or acting in the capacity of the Chief Engineer of The Pioneer Electric Power Company) shall be referee in all cases to determine the amount or the quantity of the work which is to be paid for under this contract, and to decide all questions which may arise relative to the fulfillment of this contract on the part of the Contractor, and his estimates and decisions shall be final and conclusive; also the said Chief Engineer, by himself, or by assistants or inspectors acting for him, shall inspect the work to be done under this agreement, to see that the same is done strictly in accordance with the requirements of the specifications herein set forth.

C.

The parties further agree that wherever the words defined below are used in this contract, they shall be understood to have the meanings herein given.

Company.

The term "Company" shall mean The Pioneer Electric Power Company, or any committee duly authorized by its board of directors to represent said Company in the execution of the work covered by this contract.

Engineer.

The word "Engineer," when not further qualified, shall mean the said Chief Engineer of The Pioneer Electric Power Company, or his properly authorized agents, limited to the particular duties intrusted to them.

Contractor. The word "Contractor" shall mean the person or persons, copartnership or corporation, who have entered into this contract as party of the second part, or his or their legal representatives.

D. It is further agreed that the quantities of work to be done and materials to be furnished, as given in the accompanying Instructions to Bidders, are only for the purpose of comparing the bids offered for the work under the contract on a uniform basis; and it is hereby agreed that The Pioneer Electric Power Company expressly reserves the right to increase or diminish the above mentioned quantities, or any of them, as may be deemed necessary by the Engineer.

E. The plans and specifications are intended to be explanatory of each other; but should any discrepancy appear or any misunderstanding arise as to the import of anything contained in either, the parties hereto further agree that the explanation and decision of the Engineer shall be final and binding to the Contractor; and all directions and explanations required, alluded to, or necessary to complete any of the provisions of this

Plans. contract and specifications and give them due effect, shall be given by the said Engineer. Corrections of errors or omissions in drawings or specifications may be made by the said Engineer, when such corrections are necessary for the proper fulfillment of the intention of such drawings or specifications, the effect of such corrections to date from the time that the said Engineer gives due notice thereof to said Contractor.

F. It is further agreed that the Engineer may make alterations in the line, grade, plan, form, position, dimensions or material of the work herein contemplated, or of any part thereof, either before or after the commencement of construction. If such alterations diminish the quantity of work to be done, they shall not constitute a claim for damages, or for anticipated profits

Alterations. on the work that may be dispensed with; if they increase the amount of work, such increase shall be paid for according to the quantity actually done, and at the price established for such work under this contract; or, in case there is no price established, it shall be paid for at its actual reasonable cost, plus fifteen per cent. of said cost.

18

G. The drawings referred to in these specifications are eight in number, signed by the Chief Engineer, and dated

————————————————————————————————

Plans. They show the location of the work and its general character. During the progress of the work, such working plans will be furnished from time to time by the Engineer as he may deem necessary.

Test pits and borings have been made to ascertain the position of the bedrock at the site of the work and the character of the materials overlying it; should the character, location and extent of the various materials be found to differ from what is indicated by the test pits and borings, the Contractor shall have no claim on that account, and it is expressly understood that the Company does not warrant the indications of the tests, as noted on the plans, to be correct.

The dam is to be erected across the Ogden River Valley, at a point about eight hundred feet below the mouth of Wheeler Canyon. It will be about three hundred and forty feet long, **General** sixty feet high above the river bed, with thirty or forty feet of **Description** foundations Its foundations will be carried down to solid rock and into solid rock to such a depth as may be determined by the Engineer.

On the right or north bank of the river, a spillway or overflow weir of masonry will be built, approximately at right angles to the axis of the main dam and about one hundred and fifty feet in length; Its crest will be eight feet below the top of the main dam. There will be a channel connected with it, following the contour of the side hill, by means of which the water flowing over the spillway will be conducted to the bed of the river below. This channel will, as far as possible, be excavated in the bedrock.

Bids are requested on three distinct Plans, called in these specifications and in the drawings accompanying them Plans A, B and C respectively.

————

PLAN A.

ALL MASONRY DAM.

This plan provides for a masonry dam of the usual form and construction, as shown on Sheets I, II and VIII.

The entire dam and spillway are to be built throughout of un, coursed, broken range rubble masonry, built of quarry stone of regular sizes and shapes, laid with full beds and joints in Portland cement mortar.

The faces of the dam will be built of the same class of masonry as the central portion, but the best stones and those of the most regular form must be selected for the face and the joints must be closer.

Both faces must be carefully pointed with Portland cement mortar.

A stone coping, fifteen inches thick and three feet wide, shall be laid in cement mortar on either side of the roadway for the entire length of the dam and shall support the iron hand railing.

Cut dimension stone will be used only for these copings on the top of the dam and for the crest of the overflow weir, or in such other places as may be designated by the Engineer.

PLAN B.

DAM WITH CONCRETE PIERS AND ARCHES,

As Shown on Sheets III. IV. V and VIII.

This form of dam is to be built of concrete masonry, but the up-stream face will be enclosed with a thin steel plate covering, bolted to the concrete to prevent abrasion and the percolation of water.

There will be in all six separate piers and two abutments, joined together by circular concrete arches, both on the up-stream face and on the top of the piers.

The piers will be sixteen feet in thickness and the clear spans 32 feet. The extrados of the arches which support the water pressure is to be cylindrical, the external radius being everywhere equal to 25 feet. The thickness of the arches shall be 6 feet for the upper 60 feet of the dam (that is, down to elevation 4795). It shall be 7 feet for the next 20 feet in height (that is, to elevation 4775), and 8 feet from the last given elevation to the bedrock.

20

The interior surfaces of the different sections will have radii of 19, 18 and 17 feet respectively.

The arches and piers shall be built of concrete, mixed in accordance with the requirements hereinafter specified for concrete and for cement. The exact proportions of ingredients used will vary in the different parts. In general, the proportions will be one part of cement, two parts of sand, and four parts of broken stone for all arches and for that part of the piers which is within two feet of the exterior surface; also for all concrete deposited under water. In the rest of the work, the proportion will be one part of cement, to three parts of sand and five parts of broken stone.

The concrete shall be carefully rammed in forms or molds of proper shape. For the upper faces of the arches and piers, the steel plates, properly braced, shall serve as molds.

The roadway arches shall be semi-circular, the radius of the intrados being 16 feet and the thickness of the arch rings 3 feet. They shall be 16 feet in length at the springing and shall be extended to make a proper joint with the arches of the up-stream face and shall be absolutely continuous with the latter. The spandrel spaces above the roadway arches and the piers shall be filled with concrete to the level of the roadway. A stone coping 15 inches thick and 3 feet wide shall be laid in cement mortar on either side of the roadway for the entire length of the dam and shall support the iron hand railing.

Steel Plates The steel plate facing shall be everywhere $\frac{1}{4}$ of an inch in thickness. It shall cover the entire up-stream face of the dam, fitting closely to the concrete of the piers and arches, to which it will be bolted by short bolts, as indicated in the plans.

The steel plates in front of the arches shall be rolled to form a segment of a circle. The radius will be 25 feet, the versed sine 8 feet, 9 inches, and the actual length of each segment, measured on the arc, 43 feet, 2 inches.

The flat plates forming the facing of the piers shall be $10\frac{1}{2}$ feet long, making a lap joint with the curved plates. All connections between the plates shall be riveted lap splices for both the horizontal and vertical joints.

There shall be at every joint a single row of three-quarter inch rivets spaced three inches apart. They shall be carefully driven, the heads being closely pressed down with special reference to the exclusion of water.

The edges of the plates on the upper surface shall be calked, preferably by suitable machinery, so that the entire sheeting shall be strictly water-tight under the greatest hydraulic pressure prevailing. The edges of all plates must be, in the opinion of the Engineer, sufficiently smooth to allow of sufficient calking. Whenever this is not the case, they must be planed off to a smooth surface.

The plates covering the arched surface shall be as large as practicable so as to have the least number of joints. A vertical joint shall be made on the line that the arch springs from the pier, the flat plate being bent to the proper angle to make a lap joint with the curved plate.

The holes for the rivets shall be laid out with templets and shall be punched carefully so as to make an accurate fit, but they need not be reamed.

The quality of steel for the plates and rivets is given hereafter under the heading "Requirements for Steel Plates and Rivets."

The surface of the plate facing which is to come in contact with concrete shall be thoroughly cleaned before the concrete is deposited, but shall not be painted. The outer surface must be cleaned and then coated with two coats of Paraffine P. & B. paint.

All paint of improper composition or badly applied, or applied upon surfaces which have not been properly cleaned, or where the surface has been abraded, shall be thoroughly scraped off and such surfaces repainted, as may be directed by the Engineer. Painting shall be begun and continued as fast as the riveting and calking will permit.

Method of Procedure. The method of procedure in building this form of dam will depend upon circumstances, and particularly upon the amount of ground water encountered. The Contractor will ordinarily be allowed to adopt those methods which will conduce to the greatest economy consistent with good work. Some suggestions, are, however, hereinafter given under the heading "Plan C." for his benefit in making a proposal, which appear to indicate the most practicable methods of putting in that portion of the dam which will be below the level of the ground water.

PLAN C.

DAM WITH CONCRETE PIERS AND A STEEL PLATE FACING.

As Shown on Sheets VI, VII and VIII.

This form of dam will be built entirely of concrete masonry and curved steel plates joined by rivets. The abutments at both ends of the dam will be built of concrete. Between the abutments and connecting with them, the upper face of the dam will consist of steel plates supported by concrete piers, piers being 11 feet 6 inches thick and clear span between the piers 23 feet. The piers will be connected together at the top by concrete arches supporting part of the roadway. The lower 25 feet of the steel plate face will be imbedded in a wall of concrete 15 feet thick and 25 feet high. The concrete in the abutments, toe-wall, arches, and two feet of thickness of piers along the steel plates, shall be composed of Portland cement concrete, in the proportions of one of cement, two of sand, and four of broken stone. These proportions shall also be used wherever concrete is deposited under water, and within two feet of any contact with iron work. Other portions of the concrete will be mixed in the proportion of one, three and five, unless otherwise directed. The bedrock shall be thoroughly cleaned and all cracks shall be filled with grout immediately preceding the depositing of the concrete.

The steel plate face is designed for sheets 8 feet 10 inches wide (including lap) but sheets may be made of any width to suit the manufacturer. Length of sheets for the span plate is 27 feet and for the pier plate 13 feet 6 inches. Assuming twelve plates in the vertical height, the thickness of plates numbering from the top will be as follows:

Plates Nos. 1, 2, 3, 4, 5 and 6, $\frac{3}{8}$ inch; Nos. 7 and 8, 7-16 inch; Nos. 9, 10, 11 and 12, $\frac{1}{2}$ inch.

All horizontal splices will be lap joints with a single row of rivets, 3-inch pitch. Vertical joints of plates Nos. 1, 2, 3 and 4 will be lap joints, two rows of rivets, $3\frac{1}{2}$ inches pitch in each row. Plate No. 5 same as above, but the pitch shall be 3 inches in each row. All rivets in plates Nos. 1 to 5 inclusive shall be steel, ¾ of an inch in diameter. All rivets in plates Nos. 6 to 12 inclusive will be steel, ⅞ of an inch in diameter. Vertical joints in plate No. 6 will be lap splice, two rows of rivets, 3¼ inch pitch in each row. In plate No. 7 lap joints, two rows of rivets, 2⅞ inch pitch in each row. All vertical joints in plates Nos. 8 to 12 inclusive will be made with double butt straps 10 by ¾ inches in section, with two rows of rivets on each side of the joint, 3½ inch pitch in each row.

All joints must be calked as far as possible by machine, so as to be absolutely tight under the maximum hydraulic pressure, and edges of plates and butt straps must be planed to a bevel to facilitate calking. Edges of plates not calked need not be planed.

No coating must be put on the plates until after calking and riveting is done, and every precaution must be taken to keep the plates free from rust and dirt. All plates to be in contact with concrete must be thoroughly cleaned before the concrete is deposited. Other surfaces must be thoroughly cleaned and then coated with two coats of Paraffine P. & B. paint. All paint of improper composition or badly applied, or applied upon surfaces which have not been properly cleaned, or where the surfaces have been abraded, shall be thoroughly scraped off and such surfaces repainted, as may be directed by the Engineer. Painting shall be commenced and prosecuted as fast as the riveting and calking will permit.

The Engineer may decide, in lieu of paint, to put a cement coating to a height of 25 feet above the top of the toe-wall.

The method of procedure in building the dam will depend upon ability to control subterranean water.

It is proposed first that an excavation shall be made of the whole site of the dam to as low elevation as it can be carried without the use of sheet piling. After this is done, a sheet pile cofferdam shall be sunk to bedrock for one of the piers in the middle of the river, to be designated by the Engineer. This shall be pumped out and the bedrock thoroughly examined, and such excavation made into it as may be directed.

24

The steel plate for the back of this pier shall be put in place and concrete deposited in the excavation so made and carried to such a height as the Engineer may direct.

If, upon the investigation of this pier site, such a course is deemed practicable, the steel face imbedded in the toe-wall shall be put in place for its entire length and brought above the surface of the water. The steel plate for the entire width of the dam shall then be put in place and thereafter kept above the top of the concrete.

The construction of the remaining piers can then follow.

If the above course is not deemed practicable, it is the intention to put in a cofferdam for each pier separately, and to carry them up to the elevation of the top of the toe-wall, imbedding the steel plate in concrete in each pier, but leaving the end for riveting clear by approved form of wooden protection. From the top of the toe-wall, the steel plate shall be carried up continuously, riveting of each course being done before concrete is deposited against it. Subsequently, cofferdam excavation shall be made between the piers for placing the steel plate and portion of the toe-wall in each span. If practicable, concrete will be laid in dry excavation, but it may be decided to lay it under water. The Contractor will ordinarily be allowed to adopt those methods which will conduce to the greatest economy consistent with good work, the above suggestions being made for his benefit in making Proposal.

The toe-wall being designed to exclude the water below the steel plate, if crevices are discovered which would defeat this, they shall be followed out above the dam, as directed, and stopped by excavation and concreting, as may be directed.

Work To Be Done The different parts of the work to be done under the contract may be divided as follows:

(a) Making necessary excavations in both earth and rock for stripping the site of the dam and preparing the foundations.

(b) Cleaning off the bottom of the foundations, filling up crevices and irregularities in the bottom, in accordance with the instructions of the Engineer.

(c) Doing all pumping and other temporary work necessary to keep the excavation clear of water, and taking care of the water in the river according to such methods and by such appliances as may be approved by the Engineer.

(d)   Constructing all the masonry and steel work in the dam and waste weir.

(e)   Refilling those portions of the excavations not occupied with masonry with earth excavated, or such other material as may be selected for that purpose.

(f)   Doing all necessary rock and earth excavation and masonry and concrete work necessary for the construction of a spillway and overflow channel for carrying the surplus water to the bed of the river.

(g)   In general, doing all work necessary for the entire construction of the dam and spillway, and delivering the whole structure to the Company in a completed condition, with the masonry all pointed, with the dam ready to be put into service, in accordance with the plans and these specifications.

It is, moreover, agreed and understood, that the prices for the different classes of work, as hereinafter stated (Clause Q) shall constitute full payment for the work covered by the specifications and summarized in the paragraphs last preceding.

Must Conform to Lines and Levels.
All work during its progress and on its completion must conform truly to the lines, grades and levels to be determined and given hereafter by the Engineer, and must be fully in accordance with the plans and directions which shall be given by him from time to time, subject to such modifications and additions as said Engineer shall deem necessary during the

Excess of Work or Material Must be Ordered in Writing.
prosecution of the work; and in no case will any work which may be performed, or any materials which may be furnished in excess of the requirements of this contract, or of the plans, or of the specifications, be estimated and paid for, unless such excess shall have been ordered in writing by the Engineer, as herein set forth.

METHOD OF PROSECUTING WORK.

Order and Method.
As far as consistent with the work, the order and method of prosecuting the same will be left to the discretion of the Contractor, with whom the responsibility of such order and

method shall rest; provided, however, that the Engineer shall at all times have the right to prescribe and control such order and methods with a view to safety, rapidity and economy in the execution of the work.

PROTECTIVE WORKS.

The Contractor shall be responsible for all damage done to the work by water, whether from negligence or any other cause, during the whole period of time covered by his contract. He shall do all work needed to protect his work from water; he shall erect all temporary dams, cofferdams, sheet piling, flumes, and other devices, and shall do all necessary draining and pumping. Such damage as may be caused is to be repaired by him, without cost to the Company.

The cost of furnishing the necessary appliances, of working them, and of pumping and draining, shall be included in the prices bid for the various kinds of work.

EXCAVATION.

Excavation will be paid for at five (5) different prices, viz:

Excavation for the dam, when made with sloping sides, shall be measured in accordance with slopes and base given by the Engineer, and will be paid for per cubic yard at the prices hereinafter given (Clause Q, item a).

Earth excavation for the dam, when made in vertical trench, will be paid for per cubic yard at the prices hereinafter given (Clause Q, item b).

The rock excavation for the dam will be paid for per cubic yard at the prices hereinafter given (Clause Q, item c).

The earth excavation and rock excavation for the foundation of the overflow weir and for the waste water way channel will be paid for per cubic yard at the prices hereinafter given (Clause Q, items d and e).

The prices stipulated for earth excavation shall cover the work of removing, handling, and transporting to spoil banks and for refilling of all earth, loam, clay, sand, gravel, quicksand, mud, muck, hardpan, cemented material, stones, boulders of less than one cubic yard in volume, wood, and of any other objects or substances found below the existing surface of the ground, except rock, as specified below.

Earth Excavation

The excavation shall be made in accordance with the lines and grades established by the Engineer, and the prices paid for earth excavation shall include all sheeting, bracing, and shoring required for supporting the sides of the excavation. They shall also include all pumping, ditching, and draining, and the disposal of the excavated material in spoil banks, which shall be located at such points as may be designated by the Engineer, and also for refilling such portions of the excavation as are not occupied by the masonry.

The excavation shall be made with sloping sides or in vertical trenches, as may be deemed best by the Engineer at different stages of the work. The depth at which the sloping excavations are to be abandoned and the vertical trenches are to be begun will depend on the character of the materials encountered, and cannot be fixed in advance. In any case, the shores and bracing must be so disposed as to enable a careful inspection of the rock bottom to be made, and so as to interfere as little as possible with the laying of the masonry.

The work to be done under this head consists of all the earth work necessary for refilling that part of the foundation pits not occupied by the stone work of the dam and waste weir. The material necessary for refilling shall be selected material, taken from dumps formed during the process of excavation. The Engineer shall decide upon the quality and character of the earth to be used at various places for refilling, and it must be selected and placed in accordance with his orders. Care must be taken in refilling to fill all portions of the foundation, so that no vacant spaces may remain. The price for refilling shall be included in the price paid for earth excavation.

Refilling.

28

Rock Excavation

Rock excavation is to include the excavation of all solid rock, that is, of all material which, in the opinion of the Engineer, cannot be removed by picking, and boulders of one cubic yard or more in size. It shall be measured in excavation to the lines determined by the Engineer and estimated for payment in accordance with these lines only.

In preparing the foundations, the rock shall be excavated on the bottom and sides of the valley to such depths and widths as may be necessary to secure a proper bonding and connection of the masonry to the rock, in accordance with the directions of the Engineer. It may be roughly shaped in the form of trenches or steps, if required by the Engineer.

Must Not Use High Explosives.

All excavation of rock for the foundation of the dam on the bottom and sides of the valley is to be made with black powder, and not with high explosives. Black powder may be ordered used exclusively for rock excavation where the Engineer may so designate.

Preparing Foundations.

After excavating all materials from the surface of the bedrock, the bedrock shall be excavated to the depth of one foot, or more, if necessary, to obtain rock of such character as will afford a good, firm foundation.

Across the dam site and parallel to its front face, trenches shall be excavated to the depth of two feet or more, and the toe of the dam shall be placed not less than two feet below the natural surface of the bedrock. These trenches need not be perfectly straight, but shall be excavated so as to form an irregular surface throughout the area of the foundation, to receive the bottom of the foundation walls and to resist the sliding of the whole structure upon the natural bedrock surface.

After the natural rock surface is exposed and all loose rock is removed, by picking or otherwise, from the surface, the whole area of the surface is to be scrubbed clean with wire brooms and washed with streams from a hose, to disclose any seams or fissures that may exist. If ordered by the Engineer, such seams or fissures, if found, shall be followed out by excavation until they entirely disappear, and said excavation shall be filled with concrete made of one part Portland cement and two parts sand and four parts broken stone; said concrete to be thoroughly compacted by ramming until the water flushes to the surface, and allowed to set thoroughly before walking over or any work is done upon it.

After the natural surface of the rock is prepared to receive the foundation, grout shall be thoroughly worked into all seams and fissures just before depositing the mortar, and not enough in advance of the mortar to enable it to set independently.

In such excavations of the natural rock as above described are to be laid the foundations of the dam, such foundations to be well bonded and laid in Portland cement mortar, as herein specified against the shoulder of the natural rock.

MASONRY.

To be Laid in Portland Cement Mortar. All masonry, except where otherwise specified, shall be laid in Portland cement mortar, and shall be built of the forms and dimensions shown on the plans, or as directed by the Engineer from time to time, and the system of bonding ordered by the Engineer shall be strictly followed. All beds and joints must be entirely filled with mortar or concrete, as the case may be, and the work in all cases must be well and thoroughly bonded.

Contractor Must Provide Means to Prevent Water Interfering with work. Care must be taken that no water shall interfere with the proper laying of the masonry in any of its parts. All means required to prevent water from interfering with the work, even to the extent of furnishing and permanently placing pipes for conducting water away from points where it might cause injury to the work, must be provided by the Contractor at his own expense. Under no circumstances will masonry, except concrete masonry, be allowed to be laid in water.

Care of Masonry During Hot or Cold Weather. No masonry is to be built between the 15th day of December and the 15th day of March, nor in freezing weather, except by permission of the Engineer. All fresh masonry, if allowed to be built in freezing weather, must be covered and protected in a manner satisfactory to the Engineer and, during hot weather, all newly built masonry shall be kept wet by sprinkling water on it with a sprinkling pot until it shall become hard enough to prevent its drying and cracking and, if thought necessary by the Engineer, canvas coverings must be provided.

All masonry shall be built according to the plans and instructions furnished by the Engineer, and will be estimated and paid for by the cubic yard of twenty-seven cubic feet, computing only the actual volume thereof. No constructive or conventional measurement will be allowed, any local rule or custom to the contrary notwithstanding. The Contractor will be required to furnish the materials for and to construct all masonry in all places where masonry may be required by the Engineer for the proper completion of the work contemplated.

No Constructive Measurement of Masonry Allowed.

Masonry will be classified as follows: Dimension stone masonry, rubble masonry and concrete masonry.

Dimension Stone Masonry.

Dimension stone masonry will be used only, if ordered by the Engineer, for the parapet walls and copings of the main dam and for the steps or crest of the overflow weir.

It shall be built of selected sandstone, limestone or granite, of uniform appearance and acceptable to the Engineer. The stones shall be cut to exact dimensions, and all angles and arrises shall be true, well defined and sharp. All beds, builds and joints are to be dressed, for the full depth of the stone, to surfaces allowing of $\frac{3}{8}$ inch joints at most. The face of the stones shall be rock faced, or rough pointed, or hammer dressed, at the option of the Engineer. The exposed surfaces of the cut stones are generally to be prepared with rock face. The inside surfaces are generally to be rough pointed. The tops of the copings, bridge seats, etc., will generally be hammer dressed.

Rubble Masonry.

Rubble masonry will be used for all parts of the all masonry dam (Plan A), except where dimension stone is distinctly specified, or in the foundation, where concrete may be used at the option of the Engineer.

Rubble masonry shall be laid without any attempt at regular courses. The stones shall be hard, sound, durable, of good size and form, and free from dust, dirt, or other improper substance, and from loose seams or other defects. They must have roughly rectangular forms and all irregular projections and feather edges must be hammered off before the stones are set. The beds must be good for materials of this class and must present such even surfaces that, when lowering a stone on the surface prepared to receive it, there may be no doubt that the mortar will fill all spaces. Care must be taken to select the

largest and best stones for the face work and to use the smaller
ones for filling the spaces and interstices. Each stone shall be
laid on its natural bed in a thick, swimming bed of mortar, and
thoroughly settled down in its place. Stones must be laid so
as to break joints with each other, both horizontally and verti-
cally, so as to insure the greatest bond and strength.

After all spaces and interstices are completely filled with
mortar, fragments of stones, or spalls, shall be hammered into
them. Care must be taken to prevent the formation of large
pockets of mortar alone, and to place stones of appropriate
size and shape in all spaces of considerable magnitude on
exposed faces of walls.

The quality of the beds is to regulate, to a large extent,
the size of the stones used, as the difficulty of forming a good
bed joint increases with the size of the stones.

Various sizes must be used and regular coursing must be
avoided, in order to obtain vertical as well as horizontal bonding.

The sizes of the stones used will vary also with the character of the quarries, but, especially in the places where the
Sizes. thickness of the masonry is great, a considerable proportion of
large stones is to be used.

Generally the largest stones are not to measure more than
twenty cubic feet, and they are to be used in the proportion of
about twenty-five per cent of the whole, and they must be
omitted partially or entirely if their beds are not satisfactory.
It is expected that one-quarter of the stones used will be of
such size that two men can handle them. The balance to be
composed of intermediate sizes.

If, in the opinion of the Engineer, the size and character
of the stones shall admit of it, the joints (except the beds), in-
stead of being filled with mortar may, at his request or on his
approval, be filled with concrete made as hereinafter specified,
with the exception that the component materials shall be mixed
in the proportion of one part of cement to three parts of small
stone or gravel, of such size as the Engineer shall direct, and
thoroughly rammed, care being taken to use a moderate amount
of water only which must be brought to the surface by ramming,
such filling of joints with concrete to leave no vacancies and to

be thoroughly made. If concrete is so used, the spaces left between the stones should not be less than six inches, in order that proper ramming can be obtained.

No extra compensation shall be paid to the Contractor for the use of such concrete, the cost of which is to be included in the price herein stipulated for the masonry in connection with which it is used.

Facing.

The faces of the all masonry dam (Plan A) shall be built of rubble masonry laid, in general, in the same manner as the central portion, so as to produce, as far as possible, a homogeneous mass. The soundest and best shaped stones shall, however, be selected for this work and shall be laid in such a manner as to break joints and make the best possible face. All joints for a depth of two inches shall, if necessary, be raked out clean and shall then be carefully pointed with Portland cement mortar, mixed with sharp sand in the proportion of one part of cement to two parts of sand. Great care shall be taken, especially in the up-stream face, to produce a face impervious to the passage of water.

The cost of this face stone and of the pointing shall be included in the cost of dam masonry, as hereinafter stated, (Clause Q. item f).

Concrete Masonry (Plan A).

Concrete masonry will be used in the all masonry dam (Plan A) to fill up irregularities in the bedrock foundation and in joining the masonry to the rock at the ends of the dam and also, at the option or with the approval of the Engineer, in place of mortar and spalls in the heart of the dam. For joining the foundation to the bedrock and in such other places as he may deem proper, the Engineer may, at his discretion, order the use of neat cement, in place of concrete or mortar. This shall be paid for per barrel of four hundred pounds at the price hereinafter stated. (Clause Q, items h and j).

Plans B&C

Concrete masonry in Plans B and C will be used in all parts of the structure, excepting the coping of the dam, the crest and steps of the waste weir, where cut dimension stone may be used, wherever ordered by the Engineer.

All concrete shall be made of Portland cement, sand and broken stone, of the quality hereinafter specified. There shall be two grades of concrete, paid for at different prices (Clause Q, items f and g). The proportions of the mixture by volume will be. one part of cement to two of sand and four parts of broken stone in the richer grade; and one part of cement, to three parts of sand and five parts of broken stone in the poorer grade. The grade of cement to be used in any given part of the work will be determined by the Engineer. In computing the amount of cement used in a given mixture, it shall be measured as packed in barrels, the cubic contents of a standard barrel of Portland cement weighing four hundred pounds being taken as equal to one-eighth of a cubic yard.

The volume of the sand and broken stone shall be measured when loosely packed in boxes or barrows of any convenient standard size.

A stronger mixture will be used in some parts and a weaker mixture in others, the average amount of cement used to be, as nearly as may be, as above stated.

In the lower and thicker portions of the piers and abutments, the Contractor will also be permitted to embed in the concrete a considerable portion of larger stones, not to exceed about ten cubic feet in volume. These stones shall be of proper shapes, they shall be thoroughly wet before being used and shall be so laid as to be entirely enclosed by concrete on all their surfaces. There shall be at least twelve inches of concrete between any two adjacent stones. The proportion of stones to be embedded and their size and shape shall be at all times subject to the approval of the Engineer.

The method of making all concrete shall be the following:

The sand and cement shall first be properly mixed together dry, then formed into mortar by adding a proper dose of clean water and again thoroughly mixed, whereupon the ballast, properly moistened, shall be quickly added and mixed with the mortar, either in an approved machine, or by rapidly turning over the mass with the proper tools upon a suitable platform twice or more times, as the Engineer may direct. The resulting concrete shall be free from surplus water, but thoroughly moistened throughout, and the voids between stones shall be completely filled with mortar in excess. As soon as the mixing is completed, the concrete must be deposited rapidly **Admixture** in the place where it is required and thoroughly rammed and **with Mortar** pounded, in a manner satisfactory to the Engineer, until the water flushes to the surface and all the spaces are entirely

34

filled with mortar. Should voids afterwards be discovered, the defective work is to be removed and the spaces refilled with suitable material at the Contractor's expense Any concrete mixed and left standing so as to take an initial set shall not be used in the work. In no case shall mortar or concrete that has been left standing over night be used. Care must be taken against too severe or long continued pounding, thereby forcing the broken stone to the bottom of the layer, or disturbing the incipient set of concrete. In all cases, the concrete must be allowed to set for a sufficient time after being deposited in place, before walking over or working upon its surface is permitted. The time thus required shall be determined by the Engineer.

Concrete Laid in Water.

In case it is necessary to lay concrete in water, the material shall not fall from any height, but shall be deposited in a compact mass in the allotted place by the use of such appliances as will be approved by the Engineer.

In building the concrete piers and arches (Plans B and C) great care shall be taken to obtain a thoroughly sound and uniform grade of concrete in each part of the work. The molds shall be securely and strongly built of plank at least two inches in thickness and they must be thoroughly secured in every direction by bracing, so as to insure the correct shape and position of the concrete work. The plank used shall be tongued and grooved, with a smooth surface on the inner side of the mold, and tightly fitted together, so as to leave very small joints and as finished a surface as possible.

If necessary, to prevent adhesion, the inner surfaces of the molds shall be painted with a thin coat of crude black oil.

Surface of Concrete Work.

The outer surfaces of the concrete work must be smooth and perfect, showing as few large stones and marks of the mold as possible.

Plastering of the finished wall will not be required unless the above result should not be obtained during the filling of the molds. To insure this, a portion of the mortar used in making each batch of concrete shall be retained and used, without the addition of broken stone, for those portions of the work nearest the face. In doing this, the mortar shall be piled up for each layer in a triangular heap close to the molds, thus making a bond with the central portion of the work. After the molds are filled, they shall not be removed for at least three days, or longer if necessary, and the concrete shall be sprinkled and kept wet, as long as may be deemed necessary by the Engineer, to prevent cracking.

Broken Stone.

The broken stone for concrete shall consist of fragments of durable stone, broken so as to measure no more than two inches in any direction. All this material shall be free from dust, dirt, clay, or other improper substance and, when required by the Engineer, it shall be washed before being mixed with cement mortar. Any material under $\frac{1}{4}$ of an inch in diameter, unless required by the Engineer to be screened out, shall be counted as so much additional sand and the volume of sand reduced proportionately.

Sand.

Sand shall be clean, coarse, and silicious; it must be screened and washed, if required by the Engineer, and must be subject to his approval as to fineness and other qualities.

CEMENT.

In the construction of the dam and in all other work connected with it, Portland cement is to be used, which must be of a superior quality. It shall be well packed in strong barrels of standard size, so as to be reasonably secure from air.

Vigorous and continuous tests will be made of all cements to be used. Samples may be taken from each and every barrel and a failure of one-tenth of the samples tested may be sufficient cause for the rejection of all barrels in the same lot from which the samples have been taken.

Tensile Tests.

The standard test used will be the testing for tensile strength of standard briquettes of *neat* cement, one inch square at their least section.

All cement to be accepted must conform to both of the following tests:

When left one hour in the air and the balance of 24 hours in water of a temperature of about 60 degrees, the briquette shall stand a tensile stress of at least 100 lbs. per sq. in. before breaking. When left 24 hours in the air and six days in water of a temperature of about 60 degrees, the briquette shall stand a tensile stress of at least 300 lbs per sq. in.

The degree of fineness shall be such that at least 85 per cent. shall pass through a standard No. 100 sieve, (10,000 meshes to the square inch). A cement that cracks or checks when made into thin cakes, or that begins to set in less than twenty minutes, shall not be accepted.

It must also test and act to the satisfaction of the Engineer when mixed with sand, and will be subject to constant inspection. If other than the tensile tests ordinarily made seem necessary to the Engineer, he shall have the privilege of conducting the same and, if the cement fails to pass any of them to his satisfaction, it shall be rejected. No charge shall be made for samples of cement taken for such tests. The Contractor shall at all times keep in store, at some convenient point in the vicinity of the work, a sufficient quantity of cement to allow ample time for the tests to be made, without delay in the work of construction. It shall also be stored in a tight building and each cask must be raised above the ground by blocking, or otherwise. As soon as notified of the arrival of the cement, the Engineer will cause to be made such tests as, in his judgment, may be necessary. If any cement is found of improper quality, it shall be branded, and must be immediately removed from the work.

Tests of Cement.

PLANS B AND C.

STEEL.

The treatment and manufacture of the steel plates and rivets used in the facing of this form of dam shall conform in all respects to the following requirements and to the detailed drawings to be furnished for this work.

Steel Plates and Rivets.

REQUIREMENTS FOR STEEL PLATES AND RIVETS.

The steel shall be of the class termed "soft medium" and shall be made by the open hearth process, either the basic process or the acid process, as the Engineer may determine. If made by the basic process, the percentage of phosphorus shall not exceed .04 and of sulphur not be greater than .04; if made by the acid process, it shall not contain more than .07 per cent. of phosphorus and not more than .04 of sulphur. The percentage of manganese shall not be greater than .60 per cent. Each sheet shall be uniformly homogeneous in quality, and should a reasonable doubt exist as to the quality or uniformity of the steel furnished, the Engineer may order additional tests before acceptance.

Chemical Analyses.
A sufficient number of chemical analyses of each heat or melt, to determine the quality of the steel, shall be made by the manufacturer without expense to the Company, and properly certified copies of the final analyses of the finished material, giving percentages of carbon, phosphorus, manganese and sulphur, shall be furnished to the Engineer of the Power Company, or his representative, as the work progresses.

Physical Tests.
Physical tests to determine the tensile strength, elastic limit, softness and ductility of the material of each heat or melt shall also be made at the expense of the Contractor by an experienced Inspector, whose services shall be satisfactory to the Chief Engineer of The Pioneer Electric Power Company, and who shall keep a complete record of all analyses and tests, identifying each by its respective melt number. Such record shall be open to inspection of the Engineer at any and all times.

Heat Numbers.
For the purpose of identification, the heats or melts shall be numbered consecutively and the corresponding number stamped upon each plate or sheet produced therefrom. A lack of sufficient identification may be cause for rejection of an entire heat or melt.

Test Pieces to be Furnished.
Test pieces shall be furnished from at least twenty per cent. of the finished material of each melt, but at least two test pieces shall be made from every melt. The plates or sheets from which test pieces are taken shall be selected at random by the Inspector, and each piece shall be numbered with the corresponding melt number.

Tensile test pieces shall be at least sixteen inches long and shall have, for a length of eight inches, a uniform planed edge sectional area of at least one-half square inch, the width in no case to be less than the thickness of the piece.

Bending test pieces to be twelve inches long and to have a width not less than four times the thickness, with edges planed smooth.

Punching test pieces shall be $1\frac{3}{4}$ inches wide and not less than ten inches long.

38

Drifting test pieces shall be three inches wide and not less than five inches long.

Results of Tests. Test pieces as above shall give results as follows: Ultimate strength, 55,000 pounds to 65,000 pounds. Elastic limit, not less than one-half ultimate strength. Elongation, not less than 24 per cent. in eight inches. Reduction of area at fracture, at least 48 per cent.

All fractures shall be fine, silky and free from crystalline appearance, or from indications of injurious treatment or insufficient working.

Bending test pieces shall bend double under the hammer, cold, without signs of cracking.

In punching test pieces, a row of eight holes, $\frac{3}{4}$ of an inch in diameter and $1\frac{1}{4}$ inches between centers shall be punched without any cracks.

In drifting test pieces, not less than two holes, $\frac{3}{4}$ of an inch in diameter, spaced two inches between centers, shall be punched and then enlarged by blows from a sledge hammer upon a drifting pin until said holes are $1\frac{1}{4}$ inches in diameter, without showing signs of failure or cracking on the inside of the hole or edge of the plate. Punching and drifting tests to be made cold.

The plates must also admit of cold hammering or scarfing to a fine edge at the laps without cracking, and the test pieces must furthermore withstand such quenching, forging and other tests as may satisfy the Inspector as to the temper, soundness and fitness for use of the material.

Failure of Test Pieces Any failure of test pieces, taken at random as aforesaid, to conform to the above requirements may, at the discretion of the Engineer or Inspector, cause the rejection of the entire product of the heat or melt from which such pieces are taken.

Thickness of Plates. All finished material shall be free from laminations, cracks, blisters, scale or cinder spots, and have clean edges and good surface free from bends. The plates shall be fully up to the required thickness at all points. Any plate whose thickness at any point may be found less than the required thickness by more than 1-100 of an inch shall be rejected without appeal. Plates varying more than five per cent. from the weights per square foot given in the table below, will be rejected and no allowance will be made for weights more than five per cent. in excess of the standard weights required.

TABLE OF STANDARD WEIGHTS.

THICKNESS OF PLATE.	WEIGHT PER SQUARE FOOT.
3-8 inch.	15.3 pounds.
7-16 "	17.86 "
1-2 "	20.40 "
9-16 "	22.96 "
5-8 "	25.50 "
11-16 "	28.06 "

The plates shall be rolled as flat as good mill practice will permit and each plate shall be cut to the dimensions required. A variation of more than one-fourth of an inch from the dimen-**Variation in** sions required on either length or width of plate will not be **Dimensions** permitted and in no case shall they be scant of the required dimensions. All material shall be finished in a first-class, workmanlike manner.

The Engineer of the Power Company, or his representative. shall have the right at all times to inspect the process of manufacture and testing of any and all plates, and may have, **Additional** in his discretion, an additional number of test pieces, not more **Test Pieces** than one-fourth of the whole, prepared as above from such melts as he may designate, for testing under his own supervision, at the expense of the Power Company.

It is understood and agreed that any plate that shows any defect during the process of punching, bending. or riveting shall be rejected, notwithstanding that the same may previously have been satisfactorily tested.

Rivets shall be made of a good grade of soft steel and shall have a tensile strength between the limits of 56,000 pounds and 64,000 pounds per square inch, with an elastic limit not less than 36,000 pounds and shearing strength not less than seventy-two per cent. of the ultimate strength.

Physical tests shall be made by the Inspector to determine the elongation and area at the point of fracture. In an ordinary test piece, as described above, the elongation shall be not less than twenty-seven per cent., and the reduction of area at point of fracture not less than fifty-four per cent. The material shall also be of such quality as will stand bending double and flat, before and after heating to a light yellow heat and quenching in cold water, without sign of fracture on the convex surface of the bend. All rivet material not conforming to the above requirements shall be rejected.

Rivets.

All plates and rivets must be free from rust and kept under cover from the time of manufacture of the plates. At the factory, the plates must be loaded under cover upon suitably covered cars. They must be delivered under cover at their destination and must be kept under roof and cover until ready for shipment, and in no way exposed to the weather or moisture. In case of accidental rusting, the rust must be removed from the plates before placing them in the structure for which they are intended.

Provision to be kept free from rust.

STEEL OR IRON FENCE.

On both sides of the roadway on top of the dam, for its entire length, an ornamental wrought iron or steel fence shall be built by the Contractor, but the Company reserves the right to substitute parapet walls or any other means for protection of roadway, as may be decided by the Engineer.

Company may substitute parapet walls for iron fence.

Plans for this fence shall be furnished by the Engineer.

The fence will have well braced posts, securely fastened to the coping, placed about eight feet between centres, with a close lattice work placed between the posts. The weight of the fence, including posts, will be about fifty pounds per lineal foot. It shall be painted two coats of an approved white lead paint.

The fence will be paid for per lineal foot at the price hereinafter stated, Clause Q. item (1).

GENERAL CONDITIONS.

Legal Representative The Contractor, before commencing his work, shall appoint an agent, resident within the city of Ogden, who shall be his legal representative and shall be authorized to receive notices and estimates from the Company or its Engineer and to transact, during the absence of the Contractor, any business in connection with the contract that may require prompt and immediate attention.

Suspension or termination of work provided for In case the Company should, by legal injunction, or for any other reason, be compelled to suspend, or terminate before completion, the whole or any portion of its work, payment will be made at contract prices for all work performed and for all materials shipped or delivered, but no claim for damages will be allowed or paid on account of such suspension or termination of work, or for prospective profits on uncompleted work.

Incompetent employees to be discharged. The Contractor shall employ competent mechanics for every species of mechanic's work. If any person employed by the Contractor on the work shall appear to the Engineer to be incompetent, disorderly, disobedient, or offensive, he shall be discharged immediately on the requisition of the Engineer, and such person shall not be again employed on the work.

Granding & removing rejected material. Any materials condemned or rejected by the Engineer, or his representatives, may be branded, or otherwise marked and shall, on demand, be at once removed to a satisfactory distance from the work.

Inspection of work does not relieve Contractor of his obligation. Any unfaithful or imperfect work that may be discovered before the final acceptance of the whole work, shall be corrected immediately, and any unsatisfactory material delivered shall be rejected on the requirement of the Engineer, notwithstanding that it may have been previously overlooked by the Inspector. The inspection of the work shall not relieve the Contractor of any of his obligations to perform sound work, as herein prescribed; and all work of whatever kind which, during its progress and before its final acceptance, may become damaged from any cause, shall be removed and be replaced by good satisfactory work, at the expense of the Contractor.

42

If found necessary, the Contractor shall erect and maintain fences along the roadways and around the grounds occupied by him. These fences must be of such character as to be sufficient, in the opinion of the Engineer, for the prevention of accident to people driving along the highway, or for the protection of property.

Fences for protection of property and prevention of accident.

The Contractor shall give all necessary facilities to employees of the Bear River Irrigation & Ogden Water Works Company for performing work which may be adjoining his own; also to The Pioneer Electric Power Company, or its employees, and to other contractors, for performing any and all work which the said Company may have in hand.

Contractor to give facilities to other employees.

Whenever the Contractor is not present on any part of the work where it may be deemed necessary to give directions, orders may be given by the Engineer or his agent to the superintendent or foreman who may have charge of the particular work in question, and such orders shall be obeyed.

Orders given foremen must be obeyed.

All lines and grades are to be given by the Engineer, who may change them from time to time wherever, in his judgment, a change may be necessary, and such lines and grades must be carefully observed by the Contractor. Stakes and marks given by the Engineer must be carefully preserved by the Contractor, and the Contractor must give the Engineer all necessary assistance and facilities for establishing benches, etc., and for making measurements.

Contractor must preserve stakes and benches

In all of the operations connected with the work herein specified, all laws or regulations of the State of Utah and the County of Weber controlling or limiting in any way the actions of those engaged on the works, or affecting the methods of doing the work shall be complied with and the Contractor shall provide such precautions as may be necessary to protect life and property.

Local and State laws must be complied with

Precaution to protect life and property

After the completion of the work, the Contractor is to remove all temporary structures built by him and all surplus materials of all kinds from the site of the work, and to leave the grounds about the work in neat condition, in such manner as may be directed by the Engineer.

Temporary structures and materials must be removed.

43

H.

Subletting work.

The Contractor agrees that he will give his personal attention to the fulfillment of this contract; and that he will not sublet the aforesaid work, but will keep the same under his control, and that he will not assign, by power of attorney or otherwise, any portion of the said work, unless by and with the previous consent of the Chief Engineer of The Pioneer Electric Power Company, to be signified by endorsement on this agreement.

I.

Ways and means.

The Contractor shall furnish the necessary scaffolding, ways, and all necessary means and conveniences, for the proper transfer of the material to its proper place and for its erection. And it is also to be understood that the Company shall not be held responsible for the care or protection of any materials or parts of the work until its final acceptance.

J.

Access to Work.

It is agreed that the Engineer, or his authorized agents and assistants, shall at all times have access to the work during its progress, and shall be furnished with every reasonable facility for ascertaining that the work being done is in accordance with the requirements and intention of this contract.

K.

Alterations of Work.

Should it be found desirable by the Company to make alterations in the form or character of any of the work, the Company may order such alterations to be made, defining them in writing and in drawings, and they shall be made accordingly; provided, that in case such changes increase the cost of the work, the Contractor shall be fairly remunerated; and, in case they shall diminish the cost of the work, a proper deduction from the contract price shall be made; the amount to be paid or deducted to be decided by the Engineer.

L.

Extra work.

The Contractor hereby agrees that he will do such extra work as may be required by the Engineer for the proper construction and completion of the whole work herein contemplated; that he will make no claims for extra work unless it shall have been done in obedience to a written order from the said Engineer, or his duly authorized agent; that all claims for extra work done in any month shall be filed in writing with the Engineer before the second day of the following month; and that, failing to file such claims within the time required, all right for pay for such extra work shall be forfeited. The price

44

to be paid for all extra work done shall be its actual reasonable cost to the Contractor, as determined by the Engineer, plus fifteen per cent. of said cost.

M.

Appliances. The Contractor is to use such appliances for the performance of all the operations connected with the work embraced under this contract as will secure a satisfactory quality of work and a rate of progress which, in the opinion of the Engineer, will secure the completion of the work within the time herein specified. If, at any time before the commencement or during the progress of the work, such appliances appear to the Engineer to be inefficient or inappropriate for securing the quality of work required or the said rate of progress, he may order the Contractor to increase their efficiency or to improve their character, and the Contractor must conform to such order; but the failure of the Engineer to demand such increase of efficiency or improvement shall not relieve the Contractor from his obligation to secure the quality of work and the rate of progress established in these specifications.

N.

Delays or violations of agreement The Contractor further agrees that, if the work to be done under this contract shall be abandoned by him, or if at any time the Engineer shall be of the opinion, and shall so certify in writing to the board of directors of the Company, that the said work is unnecessarily or unreasonably delayed, or that the said Contractor is wilfully violating any of the conditions or agreements of this contract, or is not executing said contract in good faith, or fails to show such progress in the execution of the work as will give reasonable grounds for anticipating its completion within the required time, the Company shall have power to notify the Contractor to discontinue all work, or any part thereof, under this contract; and thereupon the said Contractor shall cease to continue said work, or such part thereof as the Engineer may designate; and the said Company shall thereupon have the right at its discretion to contract with other parties for the delivery or completion of all or any part of the work left uncompleted by the Contractor, or for the correction of the whole or any part of said work. And, in case the expense so incurred by the Company is less than the sum which would have been payable under this contract if the same had been completed by the Contractor, then the Contractor shall be entitled to receive the difference; and in case such expense shall exceed the last said sum, then the Contractor shall,

on demand, pay the amount of such excess to the Company, on
notice from the Company of such excess so due; but such excess to be paid by the Contractor shall not exceed the amount
of the security for the performance of this contract.

O.   The Contractor agrees, in consideration of the premises,
that no liens of material men, workmen, or other persons shall
be made or filed against any of the premises or property of the
Company by any person or persons furnishing material for or
engaged upon the work of said dam or its appurtenances, and
all material used in the construction of said dam shall be free
and clear of any and all claims or liens of manufacturers, or
material men or laborers, when the same is placed upon the
grounds and premises of the Company, and so soon as such
material for the use and construction of said dam is placed
upon the grounds of the Company for use in the construction
thereof, or any of its appurtenances, the title to such property
and material shall at once vest in the Company, subject to the
right of the Contractor to receive his fair compensation under
this contract therefor.

Claims Against Contractor for material or labor.

The said Contractor further agrees that the Company
may, if it deem it expedient so to do, retain out of any amount
due the Contractor sums sufficient to cover any unpaid claims
of mechanics or laborers for work or labor performed under
this contract, or for material entering into the work, either directly or indirectly; provided, that notice in writing of such
claims, signed by the claimants, shall have been previously
filed in the office of the Engineer.

P.

Contractor agrees to indemnify the Company.

The said Contractor further agrees that he will indemnify
and save harmless the Company from all claims against said
Company, under the laws of the State of Utah, with reference
to liens on buildings and lands, for labor done and materials
furnished under this contract, and shall furnish the Company
with satisfactory evidence, when called for by them, that all
persons who have done work or furnished materials under this
contract, for which the Company may become liable, and all
claims from private corporations, or individuals, for damage of
any kind caused by the construction of said work, have been
fully paid or satisfactorily secured; and in case such evidence
is not furnished, an amount necessary and sufficient to meet
the claims of the persons or corporations aforesaid, shall be

46

retained from any moneys due, or that may become due the said Contractor under this contract, until the liabilities aforesaid shall be fully discharged or satisfactorily secured.

The Contractor further agrees that he will indemnify and save harmless the Company from all suits or actions, of every name and description, brought against the Company for or on account of any injuries or damages received or sustained by any person or persons, by or from the said Contractor, his servants or agents, in the construction of said work, or by or in consequence of any negligence in guarding the same, or any improper materials used in its construction, or by or on account of any act or omission of the Contractor or his agents; and the said Contractor further agrees that so much of the money due him under and by virtue of this agreement as shall be considered necessary by the Engineer, may be retained by the Company until all such suits or claims for damages as afore said shall have been settled, and evidence to that effect furnished to the satisfaction of the Engineer.

Q.	And the Contractor further agrees to receive the following prices as full compensation for furnishing all the materials and for doing all the work contemplated and embraced in this agreement; also, for all loss or damage arising out of the nature of the work aforesaid, or from the action of the elements, or from any unforseen obstructions or difficulties which may be encountered in the prosecution of the same, and for all risks of every description connected with the work; also, for all expense incurred by or in consequence of the suspension or discontinuance of said work, as herein specified, and for well and faithfully completing the work, and the whole thereof, in the manner and according to the plans and specifications, and the requirements of the Engineer under them, to-wit:

PLAN A.

ALL MASONRY DAM.

(a)	For the earth excavation required for the foundation of the dam, slopes 1 to 1, including all timber necessary for shoring and bracing, and all labor and material necessary for pumping and draining, as hereinbefore specified, and includ-

47

ing the refilling with approved material of all spaces in the excavation not occupied by the masonry, the sum of ....
....dollars, $.................., per cu. yd.

(b)   For the rock excavation required for the foundation and sides of the dam, and all work incidental thereto, the sum of ....dollars, $..................., per cu. yd.

(c)   For the earth excavation required for the foundation of the overflow weir and in making a channel for the waste water from the overflow weir, and all work incidental thereto, the sum of...dollars, $..................., per cu. yd.

(d)   For the rock excavation required for the foundation of the overflow weir and in making a channel for the waste water from the overflow weir, and all work incidental thereto, the sum of..dollars, $..................., per cu. yd.

(e)   For the rubble masonry in the dam and overflow weir, to comprise all the masonry (excepting only such cut dimension stone masonry as may be ordered for copings, etc., and such concrete masonry and neat cement as may be required for leveling up the bedrock and joining it to the dam) as hereinbefore specified, and all work incidental thereto, the sum of
....dollars, $..................., per cu. yd.

(f)   For concrete in place, made with Portland cement, sand and broken stone, in the proportions of one, two and four by volume, as hereinbefore specified, together with all work incidental thereto, the sum of..dollars, $.................. per cu. yd.

(g)   For concrete in place, made with Portland cement, sand and broken stone, in the proportions of one, three and five by volume, as hereinbefore specified, together with all work incidental thereto, the sum of..dollars, $.................. , per cu. yd.

(h)   For Portland cement, to be used neat when ordered by the Engineer, per barrel of four hundred pounds, the sum of ....dollars, $..................., per bbl.

48

(j)   For cut dimension stone masonry laid in Portland cement mortar, as hereinbefore specified, to be used for copings and the crest of the overflow weir, etc., the sum of__ _____ dollars, $............., per cu. yd.

(k)   For ornamental wrought iron or steel railing, four feet high, for roadway, riveted up in place, the sum of_____ _____ _____ _____ _____ dollars, $........ .------. per lin. ft.

(l)   For all extra work done by the written order of the Engineer, its actual reasonable cost to the Contractor, as determined by the Engineer, plus fifteen per cent of said cost.

PLAN B.

Dam with Piers and Concrete Arches.

(a)   For earth excavation with sloping sides, slopes 1 to 1, required for the foundation of the dam, including all timber necessary for shoring and bracing, and all labor and material necessary for pumping and draining, as hereinbefore specified, and including the refilling with approved material of all spaces in the excavation not occupied by the masonry and steel, the sum of _____ _____ dollars, $........ .------. per cu. yd.

(b)   For earth excavation in vertical trenches, required for the foundation of the dam, including all timber necessary for shoring and bracing, and all labor and material necessary for pumping and draining, as hereinbefore specified, and including the refilling with approved material of all spaces in the excavation not occupied by masonry and steel the sum of_____ _____ _____ ....dollars, $............. per cu. yd.

(c)   For the rock excavation required for the foundation and sides of the dam, and all work incidental thereto, the sum of _____ _____dollars, $.............., per cu. yd.

(d)   For the earth excavation required for the foundation of the overflow weir and in making a channel for the waste water from the overflow weir, and all work incidental thereto, the sum of_____ _____ .... dollars, $........ .------., per cu. yd.

(e)   For the rock excavation required for the foundation of the overflow weir and in making a channel for the waste water from the overflow weir, and all work incidental thereto, the sum of ....dollars, $................, per cu. yd.

(f)   For concrete in place, made with Portland cement, sand and broken stone, in the proportions of one, two and four by volume, as hereinbefore specified, together with all work incidental thereto, the sum of...dollars, $................, per cu. yd.

(g)   For concrete in place, made with Portland cement, sand and broken stone, in the proportions of one, three and five by volume, as hereinbefore specified, together with all work incidental thereto, the sum of...dollars, $................, per cu. yd.

(h)   For Portland cement, to be used neat where ordered by the Engineer, per barrel of four hundred pounds, the sum of ....dollars, $................, per cu. yd.

(j)   For steel plate work for the facing, including butt straps, angle irons and angle bracing, riveted in place, including field rivets, the sum of...dollars, $................, per pound of finished material.

(k)   For cut dimension stone masonry, laid in Portland cement mortar, as hereinbefore specified, to be used for copings, the crest of the overflow weir, etc., the sum of..dollars, $................, per cu. yd.

(l)   For ornamental wrought iron or steel railing, four feet high, for roadway, riveted up in place, the sum of..dollars, $................, per lin. ft.

(m)   For all extra work done by the written order of the Engineer, its actual reasonable cost to the Contractor, as determined by the Engineer, plus fifteen per cent. of said cost.

50

PLAN C.

COMBINATION DAM WITH CONCRETE PIERS AND A
STEEL PLATE FACING.

(a) For earth excavation with sloping sides, slopes 1 to 1, required for the foundation of the dam, including all timber necessary for shoring and bracing, and all labor and material necessary for pumping and draining, as hereinbefore specified, and including the refilling with approved material of all spaces in the excavation not occupied by the masonry and steel, the sum of......... ....dollars, $................. , per cu. yd.

(b) For earth excavation in vertical trenches, required for the foundation of the dam, including all timber necessary for shoring and bracing, and all labor and material necessary for pumping and draining, as hereinbefore specified, and including the refilling with improved material of all spaces in the excavation not occupied by masonry and steel, the sum of......... ....

....dollars, $................. , per cu. yd.

(c) For the rock excavation required for the foundation and sides of the dam, and all work incidental thereto, the sum of

....dollars, $................, per cu. yd.

(d) For the earth excavation required for the foundation of the overflow weir and in making a channel for the waste water from the overflow weir, and all work incidental thereto, the sum of...... ....__ dollars, $...... ...., per cu. yd.

(e) For the rock excavation required for the foundation of the overflow weir and in making a channel for the waste water from the overflow weir, and all work incidental thereto, the sum of.............................. ....dollars, $............... , per cu. yd.

(f) For concrete in place, made with Portland cement, sand and broken stone, in the proportions of one, two and four by volume, as hereinbefore specified, together with all work incidental thereto, the sum of............................. .... dollars, $.............. per cu. yd.

(g)   For concrete in place, made with Portland cement, sand and broken stone, in the proportions of one, three and five by volume, as hereinbefore specified, together with all work incidental thereto, the sum of.. dollars, $............., per cu. yd.

(h)   For Portland cement, to be used neat where ordered by the Engineer, per barrel of four hundred pounds, the sum of .... dollars, $............., per bbl.

(j)   For steel plate work for the facing, including butt straps, angle irons, I beams, buckle plates and angle bracing, riveted in place, including field rivets, the sum of.................................... .... -, $..............., per pound of finished material.

(k)   For cut dimension stone masonry, laid in Portland cement mortar, as hereinbefore specified, to be used for copings, the crest of the overflow weir, etc., the sum of....... .... dollars, $............., per cu. yd.

(l)   For ornamental wrought iron or steel railing, four feet high, for roadway, riveted up in place, the sum of.................. ....dollars, $............., per lin. ft.

(m)   For all extra work done by written order of the Engineer, the actual reasonable cost to the Contractor, as determined by the Engineer, plus fifteen per cent. of said cost.

. R.   And it is further agreed that payment for the work embraced in this contract shall be made in the following manner:

A payment will be made, on or about the 15th day of each month, of eighty-five per cent. of the value of the work completed in place by the Contractor on the last day of the previous month, as estimated by the Engineer; provided, however, that the making of such payment may be deferred from month to month when, in the opinion of the Engineer, the value of work done since the last estimate for payment is less than One Thousand ($1,000.00) Dollars.

Method and conditions of payment.

The said Contractor further agrees that he shall not be entitled to demand or receive final and full payment, for any one of the aforesaid classes of work or materials, until the whole work described in this contract and specifications shall have been fully completed to the satisfaction of the Engineer, and the said Engineer shall have given his certificate to that effect; whereupon the Company will, within sixty days after such completion and the delivery of such certificate, pay the said Contractor the whole amount of money accruing to the said Contractor under this contract, except such sum or sums as may be lawfully retained by said Company under this contract; provided, that nothing herein contained be construed to affect the right hereby reserved of the said Company to reject the whole or any portion of the aforesaid class of work, should the said certificate be found or known to be inconsistent with the terms of this agreement, or otherwise improperly given.

S.

Contract to be in triplicate.

The parties hereto further agree that this contract shall be in writing or in printed form, and executed in triplicate, one of which triplicates shall be kept by the Engineer, one to be delivered to the Treasurer of the Company, and one to the Contractor; that this contract shall be utterly void as to the Company if any person holding any office in said Company is either directly or indirectly interested therein.

Bond.

And the said Contractor further agrees that he will execute a bond in the sum of Fifty Thousand ($50,000.00) Dollars, and with such sureties as shall be approved by the Executive Committee of the Board of Directors of The Pioneer Electric Power Company, to keep and perform well and truly all the terms and conditions of this contract on his part to be kept and performed, and to indemnify and save harmless the said Company, as herein stipulated.

T.

And it is also to be understood and agreed that, in case of any alterations, so much of this agreement as is not necessarily affected by such alterations shall remain in force upon the parties hereto.

U.

And the said Contractor hereby further agrees that the payment of the final amount due under this contract and the adjustment and payment of the bills rendered for work done in accordance with any alterations of the same, shall release the Company from any and all claims or liability on account of work performed under this contract, or any alteration thereof.

IN WITNESS WHEREOF, the parties to these presents have hereunto set their hands and seals the day and year first above written.

SIGNATURE

WITNESS TO SIGNATURE:

If Corporation, sign by President and Secretary and affix seal of Co.

www.ingramcontent.com/pod-product-compliance
Lightning Source LLC
Chambersburg PA
CBHW021642270326
41931CB00008B/1125

* 9 7 8 3 3 3 7 4 0 2 3 2 7 *